PROBLEM SOLVING

THE PROS & CONS METHOD

Rave Review Books

Using The Pros & Cons Method

If you have a decision in your life that is important and not as easy as a yes or no, here is a simple method to help. Thinking of a new job, buying a home or renting, moving to a new town or state, whom to vote for or something like planning a vacation.

Using the pros and cons method will aid you in making the best decision by eliminating your emotions from the equation using both sides the benefits and the drawbacks to come to a decision.

The Simple Formula for Making Your Decisions

Using the book is easy. One column contains all the pros and the other contains all the cons.

You can visually see that one column ends up longer than the other, so it becomes obvious that either the pros win over the cons or the other way around. Using this method and writing down the pros and cons you focus your brain to see clearly what the good points and the bad points are about your decision you need to make and decide accordingly.

An easy method to help solve that problem is to make the list much more enlightening, by adding an algorithmic technique to the decision-making process:

- **Once you completed the list, you should analyze it and apply an estimated weight to each pro or con.**
- **Then you can strike out two items with the same weight.**
- **Continue by removing from the list all the items where one pro would equal in weight two cons. That eliminated three items.**
- **Then do the same in reverse by removing all items where two cons equal three pros. That would be five more items eliminated.**
- **By using this process it will reduce the list to a more manageable size and leaving only the most important items to consider for making the ultimate decision.**
- **You are now on your way to making an informed decision.**

THE PROS & CONS METHOD

Weight	The Pros	Weight	The Cons

The Solution:

The Pros & Cons Method

Weight	The Pros	Weight	The Cons

The Solution:

The Pros & Cons Method

Weight	The Pros	Weight	The Cons

The Solution: ____________________

The Pros & Cons Method

Weight	The Pros	Weight	The Cons

The Solution:

The Pros & Cons Method

Weight	The Pros	Weight	The Cons

The Solution:

The Pros & Cons Method

Weight	The Pros	Weight	The Cons

The Solution:

The Pros & Cons Method

Weight	The Pros	Weight	The Cons

The Solution:

The Pros & Cons Method

Weight	The Pros	Weight	The Cons

The Solution:

The Pros & Cons Method

Weight	The Pros	Weight	The Cons

The Solution:

THE PROS & CONS METHOD

Weight	The Pros	Weight	The Cons

The Solution:

The Pros & Cons Method

Weight	The Pros	Weight	The Cons

The Solution:

The Pros & Cons Method

Weight	The Pros	Weight	The Cons

The Solution:

The Pros & Cons Method

Weight	The Pros	Weight	The Cons

The Solution:

THE PROS & CONS METHOD

Weight	The Pros	Weight	The Cons

The Solution: ______________________________

The Pros & Cons Method

Weight	The Pros	Weight	The Cons

The Solution: ______________________________

The Pros & Cons Method

Weight	The Pros	Weight	The Cons

The Solution:

The Pros & Cons Method

Weight	The Pros	Weight	The Cons

The Solution:

The Pros & Cons Method

Weight	The Pros	Weight	The Cons

The Solution:

The Pros & Cons Method

Weight	The Pros	Weight	The Cons

The Solution:

The Pros & Cons Method

Weight	The Pros	Weight	The Cons

The Solution:

The Pros & Cons Method

Weight	The Pros	Weight	The Cons

The Solution:

The Pros & Cons Method

Weight	The Pros	Weight	The Cons

The Solution:

The Pros & Cons Method

Weight	The Pros	Weight	The Cons

The Solution:

The Pros & Cons Method

Weight	The Pros	Weight	The Cons

The Solution:

The Pros & Cons Method

Weight	The Pros	Weight	The Cons

The Solution:

The Pros & Cons Method

Weight	The Pros	Weight	The Cons

The Solution:

The Pros & Cons Method

Weight	The Pros	Weight	The Cons

The Solution:

The Pros & Cons Method

Weight	The Pros	Weight	The Cons

The Solution:

The Pros & Cons Method

Weight	The Pros	Weight	The Cons

The Solution:

The Pros & Cons Method

Weight	The Pros	Weight	The Cons

The Solution:

The Pros & Cons Method

Weight	The Pros	Weight	The Cons

The Solution:

The Pros & Cons Method

Weight	The Pros	Weight	The Cons

The Solution:

The Pros & Cons Method

Weight	The Pros	Weight	The Cons

The Solution:

The Pros & Cons Method

Weight	The Pros	Weight	The Cons

The Solution:

The Pros & Cons Method

Weight	The Pros	Weight	The Cons

The Solution:

The Pros & Cons Method

Weight	The Pros	Weight	The Cons

The Solution:

The Pros & Cons Method

Weight	The Pros	Weight	The Cons

The Solution:

THE PROS & CONS METHOD

Weight	The Pros	Weight	The Cons

The Solution:

The Pros & Cons Method

Weight	The Pros	Weight	The Cons

The Solution:

The Pros & Cons Method

Weight	The Pros	Weight	The Cons

The Solution:

The Pros & Cons Method

Weight	The Pros	Weight	The Cons

The Solution:

The Pros & Cons Method

Weight	The Pros	Weight	The Cons

The Solution:

The Pros & Cons Method

Weight	The Pros	Weight	The Cons

The Solution:

The Pros & Cons Method

Weight	The Pros	Weight	The Cons

The Solution: ______________________________

The Pros & Cons Method

Weight	The Pros	Weight	The Cons

The Solution:

THE PROS & CONS METHOD

Weight	The Pros	Weight	The Cons

The Solution:

The Pros & Cons Method

Weight	The Pros	Weight	The Cons

The Solution:

THE PROS & CONS METHOD

Weight	The Pros	Weight	The Cons

The Solution:

The Pros & Cons Method

Weight	The Pros	Weight	The Cons

The Solution:

The Pros & Cons Method

Weight	The Pros	Weight	The Cons

The Solution:

The Pros & Cons Method

Weight	The Pros	Weight	The Cons

The Solution:

THE PROS & CONS METHOD

Weight	The Pros	Weight	The Cons

The Solution:

The Pros & Cons Method

Weight	The Pros	Weight	The Cons

The Solution:

THE PROS & CONS METHOD

Weight	The Pros	Weight	The Cons

The Solution:

THE PROS & CONS METHOD

Weight	The Pros	Weight	The Cons

The Solution:

The Pros & Cons Method

Weight	The Pros	Weight	The Cons

The Solution:

The Pros & Cons Method

Weight	The Pros	Weight	The Cons

The Solution:

THE PROS & CONS METHOD

Weight **The Pros** **Weight** **The Cons**

The Solution:

The Pros & Cons Method

Weight	The Pros	Weight	The Cons

The Solution:

The Pros & Cons Method

Weight	The Pros	Weight	The Cons

The Solution:

The Pros & Cons Method

Weight	The Pros	Weight	The Cons

The Solution:

The Pros & Cons Method

Weight	The Pros	Weight	The Cons

The Solution:

The Pros & Cons Method

Weight	The Pros	Weight	The Cons

The Solution: ______________________________

The Pros & Cons Method

Weight	The Pros	Weight	The Cons

The Solution:

THE PROS & CONS METHOD

Weight	The Pros	Weight	The Cons

The Solution:

The Pros & Cons Method

Weight	The Pros	Weight	The Cons

The Solution:

The Pros & Cons Method

Weight	The Pros	Weight	The Cons

The Solution:

The Pros & Cons Method

Weight	The Pros	Weight	The Cons

The Solution:

The Pros & Cons Method

Weight	The Pros	Weight	The Cons

The Solution:

The Pros & Cons Method

Weight	The Pros	Weight	The Cons

The Solution:

The Pros & Cons Method

Weight	The Pros	Weight	The Cons

The Solution:

The Pros & Cons Method

Weight	The Pros	Weight	The Cons

The Solution:

The Pros & Cons Method

Weight	The Pros	Weight	The Cons

The Solution:

The Pros & Cons Method

Weight	The Pros	Weight	The Cons

The Solution:

The Pros & Cons Method

Weight	The Pros	Weight	The Cons

The Solution:

The Pros & Cons Method

Weight	The Pros	Weight	The Cons

The Solution:

The Pros & Cons Method

Weight	The Pros	Weight	The Cons

The Solution:

THE PROS & CONS METHOD

Weight	The Pros	Weight	The Cons

The Solution:

The Pros & Cons Method

Weight	The Pros	Weight	The Cons

The Solution:

The Pros & Cons Method

Weight	The Pros	Weight	The Cons

The Solution:

The Pros & Cons Method

Weight	The Pros	Weight	The Cons

The Solution:

The Pros & Cons Method

Weight	The Pros	Weight	The Cons

The Solution:

The Pros & Cons Method

Weight	The Pros	Weight	The Cons

The Solution:

The Pros & Cons Method

Weight	The Pros	Weight	The Cons

The Solution:

THE PROS & CONS METHOD

Weight	The Pros	Weight	The Cons

The Solution:

The Pros & Cons Method

Weight	The Pros	Weight	The Cons

The Solution:

The Pros & Cons Method

Weight	The Pros	Weight	The Cons

The Solution:

The Pros & Cons Method

Weight	The Pros	Weight	The Cons

The Solution:

The Pros & Cons Method

Weight	The Pros	Weight	The Cons

The Solution:

THE PROS & CONS METHOD

Weight	The Pros	Weight	The Cons

The Solution:

The Pros & Cons Method

Weight	The Pros	Weight	The Cons

The Solution:

The Pros & Cons Method

Weight	The Pros	Weight	The Cons

The Solution:

The Pros & Cons Method

Weight	The Pros	Weight	The Cons

The Solution:

THE PROS & CONS METHOD

Weight	The Pros	Weight	The Cons

The Solution:

The Pros & Cons Method

Weight	The Pros	Weight	The Cons

The Solution:

THE PROS & CONS METHOD

Weight	The Pros	Weight	The Cons

The Solution:

The Pros & Cons Method

Weight	The Pros	Weight	The Cons

The Solution:

The Pros & Cons Method

Weight	The Pros	Weight	The Cons

The Solution:

The Pros & Cons Method

Weight	The Pros	Weight	The Cons

The Solution:

The Pros & Cons Method

Weight	The Pros	Weight	The Cons

The Solution:

www.ingramcontent.com/pod-product-compliance
Lightning Source LLC
Chambersburg PA
CBHW081444220526
45466CB00008B/2501
* 9 7 8 1 6 5 6 6 3 4 9 8 6 *